Taking Your Camera to RUSSIA

Ted Park

STECK-VAUGHN
ELEMENTARY · SECONDARY · ADULT · LIBRARY

A Harcourt Company

www.steck-vaughn.com

Photo acknowledgments
Cover ©Charles & Josette Lenars/CORBIS; p.1 ©Superstock; p.3a ©Keith Gunnar/FPG
International; pp.3b, 3d, 4 ©Superstock; p.5 ©Keith Gunnar/FPG International; p.8
©Superstock; p.9 ©Smith, Robin/FPG International; p.10 ©Vladimir Pcholkin/FPG
International; pp.13, 15 ©Superstock; pp.17, 21 ©Manewal, Ernest/FPG International; p.23
©Paul Chiasson/ AP/Wide World, Inc.; p.24 ©Mays, Buddy/FPG International; p.25 ©Peter
Johansky/FPG International; pp.27, 28a ©Vladimir Pcholkin/FPG International; p.28b
©Superstock; p.29a ©Smith, Robin/FPG International; p.29b ©Vladimir Pcholkin/FPG
International.

All statistics in the Quick Facts section come from *The New York Times Almanac* (2000)
and *The World Almanac* (2000).

Contents

 # This Is Russia

Russia is a huge country. Part of it is in Europe and part of it is in Asia. Russia has many mountains. It has wide, flat plains. These are known as steppes. Russia has icy places in the eastern part of the country. If you took your camera to Russia, you could take photographs of many of these places.

A view of the city of Vladivostok

Kamchatka Peninsula in eastern Russia

Russia has many interesting cities. Moscow is the largest city and the capital of Russia. St. Petersburg is another important city. Until recently it was known as Leningrad. Irkutsk is the largest city in a region of Russia known as Siberia. It is near Lake Baikal, the world's deepest lake. Vladivostok is an important port on the Sea of Japan.

This book will show you some of these places. It will also tell you much about the country of Russia. If you learn about Russia before you take your camera there, you will enjoy your visit more.

5 📷

The Place

For many years Russia was part of a group of countries that were known as the Union of Soviet Socialist Republics (USSR), or the Soviet Union. In 1991 the Soviet Union broke up into 15 independent nations. The largest of these countries is Russia. Other countries include Belarus, Armenia, and Ukraine. Most of these countries joined together to form a group called the Commonwealth of Independent States (CIS).

Russia is the world's largest country. It is almost two times the size of the United States. Russia stretches from the Arctic Ocean in the north to China in the south. From east to west the country is about 5,000 miles (8,000 km). At its most eastern point Russia is only about 50 miles (80 km) from the state of Alaska. From north to south the greatest distance is 2,480 miles (4,000 km). Russia is 6.5 million sq mi (17 million sq km).

Arctic Ocean

FINLAND

TONIA

St. Petersburg

MOSCOW

Nizhniy Novgorod

Ural Mountains

S i b e r i a

Lake Baikal

Irkutsk

Kamc
Penir

Vladivosto

Sea of

KAZAKHSTAN

CHINA

RBAIJAN

aspian
Sea

MONGOLIA

NORTH KOREA

N

CHINA

800 km

0   800 Miles

7 📷

The Ural Mountains are in the west of Russia. They roughly separate European Russia from Asian Russia. In the south are the Caucasus Mountains. These mountains form the southern border of European Russia.

Siberia is in the northern half of Asia. In much of Russia's northern areas and in most of Siberia, the earth is frozen all the time.

In Siberia there are also huge plains. These are known as steppes. In the north, the plains are frozen and without trees. This type of land is known as tundra. The tundra has a harsh climate, with long, very cold winters and short cool summers.

Siberia also has woodlands. The woodlands

Evergreen forests cover large parts of central Siberia.

The Volga River, Europe's longest river

are made up of evergreen forests. This land is known as taiga. The taiga begins where the tundra ends. Where the taiga ends, the steppes begin.

Russia has two important rivers. The Volga River is in European Russia. It is 2,293 miles (3,690 km) long. The Lena River is in Asian Russia. This river flows north to the Arctic Ocean.

9 📷

Moscow

Moscow is the capital of Russia. Although Moscow is not in the center of Russia, it is the political, art, and industrial center of the country. The Moskva River runs through the city. More than 8 million people live in Moscow, both in the city and in the suburbs that surround the city.

Red Square is a famous place in Moscow. It is in the center of the city. Parades are sometimes held there. People also gather there to celebrate official state events. Next to Red Square is a large group of buildings known as the Kremlin. A long time ago, the Kremlin was a fort where the ruler of Russia lived. Now it is the center of the government.

St. Basil's Cathedral is next to the Kremlin. A cathedral is a large church.

Moscow State University is the largest and oldest university in Russia.

GUM department store has many small stores inside the building.

St. Basil's was built in the 1500s. It has onion-shaped domes, or roofs, like many Russian churches. The outer walls are covered with colorful designs.

GUM department store is at one end of Red Square. It is the largest department store in Moscow.

Moscow has many museums, churches, and theaters. The most famous theater is the Bolshoi, where ballet and opera are performed.

Moscow has a good subway system with almost 200 stops along its routes. Most of the stations are nicely decorated.

Moscow's most famous skyscraper is not an office building. It is the home of Moscow State University.

11

 # Places to Visit

St. Petersburg is one of Russia's most famous cities. It was once the capital of Russia. Czar Peter the Great built the city in 1703. *Czar* is the Russian word for "ruler." St. Petersburg is on the Neva River and is built on more than 100 islands. At one time the city was known as Leningrad. St. Petersburg is Russia's largest seaport.

The most famous site in St. Petersburg is the Hermitage. This is a great art museum with more than three million items.

The Hermitage was once a royal palace.

Lake Baikal. More than 2,000 kinds of plants and animals live in and around the lake.

Near St. Petersburg is another famous palace. It was built by Peter the Great and is part of a big estate called Peterhof. The palace has many splendid rooms. In the gardens there are fountains and waterfalls.

Another place to visit is Lake Baikal, although it is far away from many places. Lake Baikal is located in southern Siberia and is the world's deepest lake. Its deepest part is about 5,315 feet (1,620 m).

13 📷

The People

Even though Russia is huge, not many people live there. Much of the country is so cold that few people want to live there. Because of this, Russia has only the sixth largest population in the world.

Almost 150 million people live in Russia. Most of them live in the European part of the country. Because of the extreme cold weather, people in the Asian part of Russia live very different types of lives than those who live in the part of Russia that is in Europe.

There are more than 120 different nationalities, or peoples, and they speak 80 different languages. The Russians are the largest group of people, but there are also Tatars and Ukrainians. The Russian language is the most widely used language. It is a phonetic language. This means that each letter represents a different sound. It is written in an alphabet called Cyrillic.

Asians in the eastern part of Russia

# Life in Russia

During the 20th century, Russians saw advances in science and education. Heavy industries, such as coal, oil, and steel, grew. After World War II many Russians moved to cities from the countryside to work in the factories. Many people still continue to move to cities.

Most of the people in the cities live in very large apartment buildings. Often, many members of the same family may live in just one room.

One fifth of Russians are farmers. Two fifths work in factories, and another two fifths work in service industries. Most Russian women work. Some people may have a cottage home outside the cities. These are wooden houses known as dachas.

It is expensive for people to live in the cities. People who live in Russia's countryside live very simply. Some houses may not have running water or electricity.

A dacha in the Russian countryside

Government and Religion

In 1917 Russia became a communist country. Communism is a system of government in which all industry is controlled by the state and goods are made available to the people as they need them. Also, the Communist party controlled the government.

In 1991 the USSR broke up, and Russia held its first elections. People who belonged to the Communist party won them. The Communist party is still important in Russia's government, although it no longer controls the country.

Russia is a federal republic. This means that the president, or leader, is elected. The president is the head of the country and leader of the armed forces. An assembly makes the laws. It is made up of two parts. One part is called the Council of the Federation. The other part is known as the State Duma.

The Kremlin at night

Under communism, religion was mostly banned in the Soviet Union. Today, about 5,000 churches in Russia hold regular services. Russian Orthodox is Russia's main religion. It is a branch of the Eastern Orthodox Church.

There are about 500,000 Jews living in Russia. Many people who live in the southern parts of Russia closest to central Asia are Muslims. They follow Islam, the religion begun by Mohammed. There are also Protestants, Buddhists, and some Roman Catholics in Russia.

 Earning a Living

Farming is important in Russia. However, only about 10 percent of the land in Russia can be used for farming. Under communism, the government tried to increase farming by collecting farms into large areas. These farms were known as collective farms. Today many of these farms are still very large. However, more and more of them are being broken up into smaller farms.

Barley, oats, and potatoes are major crops. Farmers are able to grow only enough to feed the Russian people. Buckwheat is another important crop. In Russia, it is called kasha. Beets are also grown.

Russia has many natural resources. Natural resources are things from nature that are useful to people. Russia is the largest producer of nickel and natural gas in the world. It is the third largest producer of oil and coal. Many of these natural resources are in Siberia, where it is too cold to get to them.

The Siberian pipeline carries natural gas to other parts of Russia and to western Europe. Timber is also an important natural resource, especially in the taiga. Often these things are exported, or sent out of the country to be sold.

Russia's most important industries are iron and steel. The car and truck industry is also important.

Today tourism is a major industry. More and more people from around the world are now visiting Russia.

Most of the farming in Russia is done in the warmer south.

# School and Sports

Children in Russia must go to school for 10 years beginning at age 6 or 7. They may leave school at 18. Students go to school six days a week. Children under the age of 14 are not permitted to work. Some students go on to college. Many people go to technical and trade schools. These schools prepare Russians for jobs that require technical skills. In Russia all schooling, even college, is free.

Swimming is a popular sport, even in cold weather. People think this helps them stay well during freezing Russian winters. Children must participate in sports at school. Hockey and figure skating are important sports in Russia. Many Russian athletes become gymnasts. Football, volleyball, and basketball are popular outdoor sports during the short Russian summer.

Russian hockey players compete in the World Cup.

 22

Food and Holidays

Russians eat simple meals. Meat is often combined with cabbage or beets into a steaming soup. In Siberia, meat-filled dumplings known as pelmeni are popular. They are often stored in the frozen ground! In the Arctic regions of Russia, people eat reindeer. A popular fish is sturgeon. Tea is drunk at many meals.

Russian bread

The most important holidays in Russia are Easter and Christmas. Christmas is celebrated later in Russia than in most countries. This is because the Russian Orthodox Church and the Christian church use different calendars.

Many Russians died during World War II. The country honors these people every May 9. The holiday is known as Victory Day.

Caviar is made from sturgeon's eggs.

25

The Future

If you took your camera to Russia, you would see a country that is changing. Many new things are happening in the country.

When Russia was part of a communist country, prices for most goods were cheap. They are now high. Also, many jobs, food, and goods are scarce. Russians often stand in line for hours to purchase goods. Then they find that the stores no longer have any stock left. Russia has been free of communism only since 1991. The Russian people are trying to get used to living more freely under the new system of government.

Russia has plenty of natural resources, but they are sometimes difficult to get to because of cold weather. And sometimes oil and gas spills have caused a great deal of damage to the environment. But Russia has many workers, and now they are being paid higher wages. Russians are also building new roads and railroads to get to their country's natural resources. In addition, links with other member states of the CIS

26

have become stronger. This increased trade should help the Russian economy.

Russians are excited about the future of their country. When you leave Russia, people will say the traditional Russian farewell. This is pronounced "Da svidanya." It means "Till we see each other again."

A Russian power station

Quick Facts About
RUSSIA

Capital
Moscow

Borders
Azerbaijan, Belarus, China,
Estonia, Finland, Georgia,
Kazakhstan, Latvia, Mongolia,
North Korea, Norway, Ukraine

Area
6,592,745 square miles
(17,075,200 sq km)

Population
146 million

Largest cities
Moscow (8,717,000 people);
St. Petersburg (4,838,000 people);
Nizhnyi Novgorod (1,383,000
people)

Chief crops
grain, sugar beets, vegetables,
sunflower seed, meat, milk

Natural resources
oil, natural gas, coal, timber

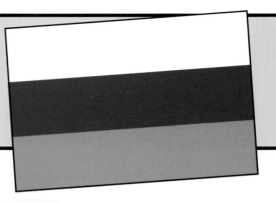

Flag of Russia

◀ **Longest river**
Volga, at 2,293 miles (3,690 km)

Coastline
23,402 miles (37,653 km)

Monetary unit
Ruble

Literacy rate
99 percent of the Russians can read and write.

Major industries
mining and processing raw materials, machines, aircraft

29

Glossary

Bolshoi (BOHL-shoy) A famous theater in Moscow where ballet and opera performances are given

Commonwealth of Independent States (CIS) A group of countries in eastern Europe, including Russia, that joined together after the Soviet Union broke up

communism (KOM-yuh-ni-zum) A system of government in which all industry is controlled by the state and goods are made available to the people as they need them

Cyrillic (su-RIH-lik) The alphabet used for writing the Russian language

dachas (DAH-chu) The Russian term for a country cottage

Irkutsk (ir-KOOTSK) The largest city in Siberia

kasha (KAH-shu) The Russian word for buckwheat

Kremlin (KREM-lun) A large group of buildings located next to Moscow's Red Square

Lake Baikal (beye-KAL) The deepest lake in the world, located in southern Siberia

 30

Leningrad (li-neen-GRAT) At one time, the name of St. Petersburg

Moscow (MAS-kow) The capital of Russia

pelmeni (pel-MEN-ee) Meat-filled dumplings

Peterhof (PEEH-tur-hof) A palace built by Czar Peter the Great near St. Petersburg

Soviet Union (SOW-vee-et) A group of countries in eastern Europe, including Russia, that joined together. The official name is the Union of Soviet Socialist Republics (USSR)

St. Petersburg A famous Russian city built on more than 100 islands by Czar Peter the Great in 1703

steppes (STEPS) Wide, flat grassy plains

taiga (TIE-guh) Woodlands made up of evergreen trees that begin where the tundra ends

tundra (TUN-druh) Frozen, treeless plains of the far north

Vladivostok (vla-duh-vuh-STOK) An important port city located on the Sea of Japan

Volga River (VOL-guh) An important Russian river and also Europe's longest river

Index